Toots and Twiddles
Classic Tunes
selected and arranged by John Loesberg

OSSIAN

Music origination, layout and design by John Loesberg.
Whistle Player by Joe Gervin.

Special thanks to Sarah Greenham and Tony O'Flaherty who proofread all tunes and suggested many improvements.

Published by
Ossian Publications
14-15 Berners Street, London W1T 3LJ, UK.

Exclusive Distributors:
Music Sales Limited
Distribution Centre, Newmarket Road, Bury St Edmunds,
Suffolk IP33 3YB, UK.
Music Sales Corporation
257 Park Avenue South, New York, NY10010, USA.
Music Sales Pty Limited
120 Rothschild Avenue, Rosebery, NSW 2018, Australia.

Order No. OMB231
ISBN 1-84609-716-9
First published 2006

www.musicsales.com

'With the toot of the flute and the twiddle of the fiddle, O;
Hopping in the middle, like a herring on the griddle, O.
Up, down, hands aroun', crossing to the wall.
Oh, hadn't we the gaiety at Phil the Fluther's Ball.'

Percy French

Titles in this series:

Irish Tunes
Tunes For The Young
Classic Tunes
Tunes Allsorts
A World Of Tunes
American Tunes

Contents

A note on playing these tunes

I have taken care to include as many different types of melodies as possible in these small offerings of great little tunes.
Dynamics are left to to the player, or perhaps can be worked out together with a teacher. Freedom is the keyword here!
Metronome indications have been left deliberately on the slow side, while never so slow that the music suffers from it. Please feel free to experiment with all aspects of the music. Chords have been applied with a sense of economy as well; extra or different chords may, of course, be inserted.
It is my hope that these musical morsels may stimulate your musical journey through life, whether as nothing more than a handy source of good tunes or perhaps as an introduction to playing from an entirely different repertory from what you are used to.
Have fun!

John Loesberg

Ode To Joy

Beethoven

Gavotte

Anon, 18th C.

Minuet

Bach

Canary Jig

Sanz

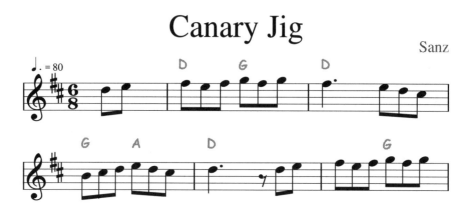

Jesu Joy Of Man's Desiring

Bach

Finlandia

Sibelius

Clarinet Concerto

Mozart

Bourree

Bach

Gavotte

Corelli

La Volta

Allegro

Byrd

Fine

D.C.

La Folia

Anon, 17th C.

Sarabande

Waltz

See The Conquering Hero

Handel

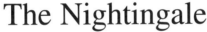

The Nightingale

Brahms

King William's March

Clarke

Prelude

Largo

Dvorak

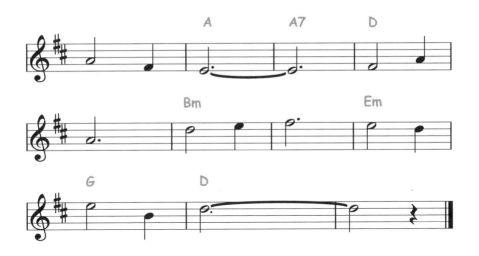

The Surprise Symphony

Andante

Haydn

Lullaby

Andante   Brahms

Melody

Andante   Tchaikovsky

Linden Tea

Vaughan Williams

Romance

Beethoven

Merry Widow Waltz

Minuet

Minuet

Handel

Andante

What If A Day

Anon, 16th C.

Vite

Telemann

Gigue

Anon, 18th C.

Fine

D.S al Fine

33

Minuet

Rigadoon

Purcell

The Sandman

Brahms

The Harmonious Blacksmith

Handel

Cantata

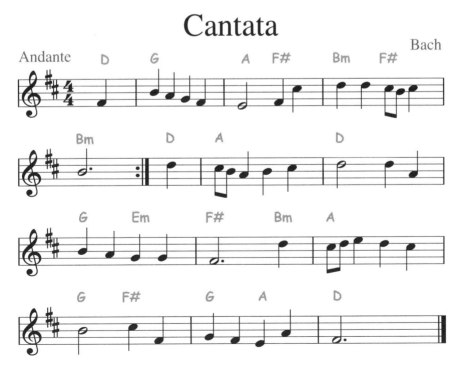

Rest Sweet Nymphs

Pilkington

123456789

Bringing you the words and the music

All the latest music in print... rock & pop plus jazz, blues, country, classical and the best in West End show scores.

- Books to match your favourite CDs.

- Book-and-CD titles with high quality backing tracks for you to play along to. Now you can play guitar or piano with your favourite artist... or simply sing along!

- Audition songbooks with CD backing tracks for both male and female singers for all those with stars in their eyes.

- Can't read music? No problem, you can still play all the hits with our wide range of chord songbooks.

- Check out our range of instrumental tutorial titles, taking you from novice to expert in no time at all!

- Musical show scores include *The Phantom Of The Opera*, *Les Misérables*, *Mamma Mia* and many more hit productions.

- DVD master classes featuring the techniques of top artists.